OUR
AMERICA

GROWING UP *in* REVOLUTION *and the* NEW NATION

1775 to 1800

BRANDON MARIE MILLER

Lerner Publications Company
Minneapolis

To Rees and Luke Chael, with love, Aunt Brandy

Lerner Publications Company
A division of Lerner Publishing Group
241 First Avenue North
Minneapolis, MN 55401 U.S.A.

Website address: www.lernerbooks.com

Library of Congress Cataloging-in-Publication Data

Miller, Brandon Marie.
    Growing up in revolution and the new nation, 1775 to 1800 / by Brandon Marie Miller.
        p.   cm. — (Our America)
    Includes bibliographical references and index.
    Summary: Presents details of daily life of American children during the period from 1775 to 1800.
    ISBN 0-8225-0078-7 (lib. bdg. : alk. paper)
    1. United States—History—Revolution, 1775–1783 —Children—Juvenile literature. 2. United States—History—Revolution, 1775–1783 —Participation, Juvenile—Juvenile literature. 3. United States—History—1783–1815—Juvenile literature. 4. Children—United States—History—18th century—Juvenile literature. 5. Youth—United States—History—18th century—Juvenile literature. 6. Children—United States—Social life and customs—18th century—Juvenile literature. 7. Youth—United States—Social life and customs—18th century—Juvenile literature. [1. United States—Social life and customs—1775–1783. 2. United States—Social life and customs—1783–1865.] I. Title. II. Series.
E209.M55   2003
973.3'083—dc21
                                                                            2001004654

Manufactured in the United States of America
  2 3 4 5 6 – JR – 08 07 06 05 04

CONTENTS

NOTE
to
READERS

Studying history is a way of snooping into the past. To gather clues about a past time, historians study things made during that time. They read old diaries and letters. They look at old newspapers, magazines, advertisements, poems, paintings, and photographs. They listen to old songs. All these things from the past are primary sources.

To write this book, the author used many primary sources. She snooped into life around the time when the United States was being formed. This time—the new nation period—covers about 1775 to about 1800.

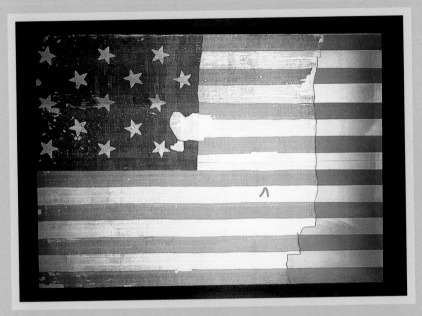

This flag has one star for each state in the United States in 1792.

Many books about this period are historical fiction. Historical fiction is a made-up story that is set in a real time. In this book, the people you will meet are real. You'll discover paintings and drawings of them. You'll find quotes from their diaries and letters. You'll notice many things that are different from modern times. For example, people of this era spelled words quite differently. Their words are printed here just the way they wrote them.

By studying all these primary sources, you'll have a chance to do some snooping of your own. Your ideas about the past can help all of us build a better understanding of it.

CHAPTER ONE

GROWING UP with WAR

"The shot of the enemy soon began to

On June 17, 1775, seven-year-old John Quincy Adams clutched his mother Abigail's hand and watched the battle in the distance. John Quincy could hear British cannon roaring over the nearby city of Boston, Massachusetts. Tears filled his mother's eyes.

The British army had seized control of Boston months ago. Since then, the prosperous city's harbor had rocked with British warships. British soldiers in bright red coats patrolled the streets. American colonists were fighting the "redcoats" (as they called the British soldiers) to win Boston back.

Across the river from Boston, the town of Charlestown was burning, and John Quincy could see the flames. Smoke choked the air.

On Breed's Hill above Charlestown, American farmers and townsmen knelt behind freshly dug barriers of earth. Shouldering guns they'd brought from home, they fired as fast as they could. Wave after wave of redcoats charged up the hill. Many fell back.

Finally, the Americans ran out of ammunition. The British stormed their position, and the Americans retreated. The British had won the battle. But both

Opposite: Colonists watch Charlestown burn in June 1775. *Above:* John Quincy Adams

pass over us like hail." —*James Collins, age sixteen, October 1780*

sides paid a heavy price. More than fifteen hundred Americans and British lay dead or wounded.

Like other young people in America in 1775, John Quincy would spend most of his growing-up years living with war. This battle, called the Battle of Bunker Hill, was one of the first in what became an eight-year-long struggle to win American independence.

◇ ◇ ◇ ◇

WHOSE SIDE ARE YOU ON?

On July 8, 1776, a crowd gathered in Philadelphia, Pennsylvania, to hear an important document read in public for the first time. The Declaration of Independence had been signed by leaders of every colony. It proclaimed: "These United Colonies are, and of Right ought to be, Free and Independent states." The United Colonies were the American colonies ruled by King George III of Great Britain. The Declaration of Independence listed the reasons why the colonists had already started fighting against Britain.

People in Philadelphia crowd close to hear the Declaration of Independence being read on July 8, 1776.

Declaring independence was an amazing act. World powers like Great Britain, Spain, France, and Russia were ruled by kings and queens. They had a class system in which rich people mostly stayed rich, and poor people mostly stayed poor.

Most Americans hoped for something different. They wanted more equality. They wanted to elect their leaders. But no one really knew how a democracy (a government run by freely elected leaders) should work.

John Quincy's father, John Adams, was one of the leaders pushing for independence. It took

"These United Colonies are, and of Right ought to be, Free and Independent states."

—Declaration of Independence, 1776

courage for him to sign his name to the Declaration of Independence. Without question, members of the Adams family were patriots (colonists who supported the revolution).

But many American families felt torn. Some remained loyal to Great Britain. Loyalists thought of Britain, which had controlled the colonies for more than 150 years, as the "mother country." Besides, Britain was so strong that a rebellion seemed doomed to fail.

Some Americans didn't choose any side. Quakers stayed neutral because the Quaker religion taught that any war was wrong. Other people waited to see what would happen.

About an equal number of Americans chose each of these three paths. But no choice was safe. British soldiers arrested any patriots they captured. And what about after the war? If Great Britain won, it might

This loyalist family was forced to flee their home.

punish patriots by seizing their money and their businesses, throwing them into jail, or executing them for treason.

Being a loyalist wasn't safe either. Patriots sometimes burned loyalists' businesses, smashed the windows of their homes, and drove them out of town covered with tar and feathers. "The people have become perfectly savage," one man wrote in a letter in 1781.

Patriots felt they had reason to distrust loyalists. After all, some loyalists worked for the British as spies. Other loyalists donated supplies to the British army. Some even joined it. Leaders in patriot towns sometimes had loyalists arrested as traitors.

Even neutral people could not avoid the war. Soldiers camped, marched, and fought in city streets and in country fields. Both armies were in constant need of horses, food, and other supplies. Soldiers simply took what they wanted from people's homes and barns.

◇ ◇ ◇ ◇

GONE TO WAR

Thousands of men and boys left home to serve in the Continental Army of the patriots. Boys as young as ten were messengers, drummers, and cooks. Older boys fought as soldiers.

Many boys like this drummer boy *(far left)* joined the patriots' army.

Battlefields were terrible places. Soldiers struggled to load their muskets (a kind of gun) quickly. Loading a musket was such hard work that the soldiers sweated and cursed. Sometimes they had to fire so fast that they kept four or five musket balls in their mouth to have the ammunition handy.

Sixteen-year-old Thomas Young fought at the Battle of King's Mountain in North Carolina on October 8, 1780. "The orders were at the firing of the first gun for every man to raise a whoop, rush forward, and fight his way as best he could," Thomas recalled. He darted from tree to tree, his eyes filled with bark sent flying by bullets.

> *"The orders were at the firing of the first gun for every man to raise a whoop, rush forward, and fight his way as best he could."*
>
> —*Thomas Young, age sixteen, October 8, 1780*

Sybil Ludington's Daring Ride

Sybil Ludington's family was getting ready for bed on April 26, 1777, when they heard a knock at the door. A messenger warned Sybil's father, a colonel in the Continental Army, that British soldiers were attacking the nearby town of Danbury, Connecticut. Colonel Ludington's soldiers were at home on their farms.

Someone had to tell the men to come to Colonel Ludington. Sybil, sixteen (shown above on her horse), knew British soldiers or outlaws might be on the dark roads. But she volunteered to go anyway. Riding her horse, Star, she hurried to farms and villages, shouting her news. Everywhere she went, her father's men hurried out the door.

Because of Sybil's courage, Colonel Ludington's soldiers kept the British from advancing that night. Later, American general George Washington came to Sybil's house to thank her.

Even without battles, army life was difficult for soldiers. Sometimes they didn't get paid. They fought in ragged clothes. Sometimes they marched shoeless. Often they went hungry. Sixteen-year-old James Collins survived by eating raw turnips and dried corn.

Some soldiers ran away. Runaways usually headed for home. They knew their families needed help with planting or harvesting.

Wounded soldiers were sent to hospitals. Sometimes their wounds got infected. Doctors had few medicines with which to heal infections. In addition, many wounded men grew sick in the hospitals. Diseases spread quickly in the filthy, overcrowded conditions. Deadly typhoid, smallpox, and dysentery killed thousands. One Delaware doctor recorded that ten to twenty soldiers died of disease for every one killed in battle.

◇ ◇ ◇ ◇

"I WILL NOT BE AFRAID OF THEM"

The Wisters were a Quaker family from Philadelphia. As their religion taught, they opposed war. But their hearts supported the patriots anyway. When the British captured Philadelphia, the Wisters fled to a relative's home in the country.

Even in the country, the Wisters couldn't escape the war. Many mornings they awoke to the sounds of rattling wagons as soldiers from one army or the other marched past the house. The beat of drums and the whistling of fifes kept the soldiers marching in time.

Once, soldiers of the Continental Army camped on the property where the Wisters were staying. Sixteen-year-old Sally Wister kept a diary. She wrote that her family was "surrounded by an Army, the house full of officers, and the yard alive with soldiers."

Days passed. The Wisters heard rumors that the soldiers were going into battle. "What will become of us?" Sally worried. "We are

During the war, no place was safe from the fighting.
This battle took place near Concord, Massachusetts in 1775.

in hourly expectation of an engagement [a battle]. I fear we shall be in the midst of it."

But Sally also enjoyed the company of the young American officers. "I feel in good spirits," she wrote. The soldiers were "very peaceable. . . men," Sally thought. "I will not be afraid of them, that I won't."

> *"What will become of us? We are in hourly expectation of an engagement [a battle]."*
> —*Sally Wister, age sixteen, 1777*

"I LONG THAT YOU SHOULD SEE THEM"

In patriot families, most fathers and older sons joined the army. Mothers and older girls took charge of things at home. They ran farms and family businesses. They refused to buy things made in Britain. They gathered supplies for the Continental Army. And they raised money for hospital work.

John Quincy Adams's father spent the war years away from home. For a while, he served in the Continental Congress (the governing body of the patriots). He also worked as a diplomat in Europe. Abigail Adams was left to run the household and to raise the five Adams children.

John Quincy was the oldest son. He felt an extra burden to help his mother. At age nine, he often rode his horse to Boston, eleven

STICKING UP FOR SLEDDING

While the British controlled Boston, they turned Boston Common (land once shared by the people of Boston) into a bustling army camp. Legend has it that a brave group of boys approached a British general (as shown in the painting below) in the winter of 1775 and 1776. How could they sled on Boston Common when the hill was covered by tents?, they asked. Impressed by their bravery, the general ordered the tents moved. No record remains to prove whether this really happened. But it's nice to imagine Boston's children sledding through the snowy whiteness on Boston Common again.

miles away. There he could pick up his father's letters to the family. The countryside was dangerous. But the ride was worth the risk, since the letters were such a comfort to his mother.

Colonial children had always had to work hard. With fathers and older brothers gone during the revolution, they pitched in even more. They cooked, spun wool, and chopped firewood. Older children cared for the younger ones. Mothers could then do the chores usually done by men. Sally Wister wrote that she got out of bed some mornings at four. She ironed until one in the afternoon. Then she baby-sat her small brother, sewed, darned socks, and studied.

Families missed their menfolk. Rebecca Silliman's husband became a prisoner of war when their son Selleck was age two and son Bennie was four months old. "They both sleep with me, and both awake before sunrise," Rebecca wrote to her husband. Seeing the boys playing together was "a sweet sight," she told him. "I long that you should see them."

During the war, both boys and girls had to do more spinning than they had done before.

"Can This Be Right?"

At the same time colonists were fighting for freedom, nearly half a million Americans were slaves. In 1779 nineteen slaves in New Hampshire asked the colony's leaders to set them free. The slaves told how they had been captured as children in Africa, brought to America, and enslaved. "Can this be right?" they wrote. "Forbid it gracious Heaven." But slavery was legal in the colonies. The New Hampshire leaders did not set them free.

To ease the sorrow of separation, many families traveled to army camps to see the family's father. The soldiers stayed in the camps while waiting for the next battle. Sometimes the camps held nearly as many women and children as soldiers.

◇ ◇ ◇ ◇

PEACE

Eight weary years of war ended with a treaty signed on September 3, 1783. The patriots and their Continental Army had won. The British agreed to leave America. By November the last British ships sailed away.

As one song put it, the world seemed to be "turned upside down." Thirteen small colonies had joined together and defeated a great power. To Great Britain, it seemed as if the child had turned on its parent. What would young America do with its hard-won freedom?

American children faced the biggest change of all. They would no longer grow up as colonists, ruled by a king on the other side of an ocean. Instead, they would be the first generation of a newborn nation—the United States of America.

CHAPTER TWO

The
WORLD
Looks toward
US

"The world looks toward us as a country that may become a great nursery of arts and science."

—*Francis Hopkinson, a signer of the Declaration of Independence, 1792*

◇ ◇

Now what? In the years after the revolution, each of the thirteen colonies eventually became a state in the United States. Almost right away, they began to argue. They wrangled over boundary lines. They squabbled over which states were most important. Hardly a proud start for the new nation!

Something had to change. In May 1787, fifty-five men gathered in Philadelphia to create a new government. The result was the U.S. Constitution. By 1788, after months of argument, nine states agreed to be governed by it. By 1790 all thirteen states had accepted the constitution. The constitution created a nation led by a congress and by a president. General George Washington was unanimously elected president. He would lead a kind of government that had never been tried before.

Opposite: People thronged to see George Washington when he arrived in New York City to be sworn in as the nation's first president on April 30, 1789. *Right:* Washington placed his hand on this Bible to take his oath of office.

The Washington family included *(from left to right)* Young Wash,
George Washington, Nelly, and Martha Washington.

THE FIRST FAMILY

In May 1789, Washington's wife, Martha, arrived in New York
from Mount Vernon, the Washingtons' home in Virginia. With her
were two grandchildren. Everyone wanted a glimpse of the new first
family. People jammed the streets to greet them.

Mrs. Washington's granddaughter, Eleanor Parke Custis
("Nelly"), was age ten. Grandson George Washington Parke Custis
("Young Wash") was eight. Their father, who had died, was Mrs.
Washington's son from an earlier marriage. Nelly and Wash saw
their mother often. But they lived with their grandparents.

The Washington family moved into a three-storied house on
Cherry Street overlooking the East River. Nelly brought her pet
parrot, Snipe, with her to the new house. She loved to sit by the
front window, watching carriages roll by. She also took dancing
lessons, since well-bred young ladies had to know how to dance.
And she worked on her "needle arts" (sewing).

Nelly liked to play her harpsichord (a keyboard instrument). But sometimes her grandmother insisted that Nelly practice for long hours. Then Nelly "would play and cry," as Young Wash later wrote. One time Nelly was invited to a friend's party. She couldn't go because she had to stay home and perform for company. Some members of the "Honorable Congress" were coming to dinner, Nelly told her friend in a letter. "They like to hear musick."

President Washington was one of the most famous men in the world. This made Nelly's friends shy. As Nelly wrote in a letter, they often "feared to speak or laugh before him." That was too bad, because President Washington liked to see Nelly "gay and happy." After joining her and her friends, he would wait a while, hoping the fun would start again. Usually everyone remained shyly silent. Then President Washington would leave, "quite disappointed."

Some members of the "Honorable Congress" were coming to dinner. . . . "They like to hear musick."

—*Nelly Custis, age ten, 1789*

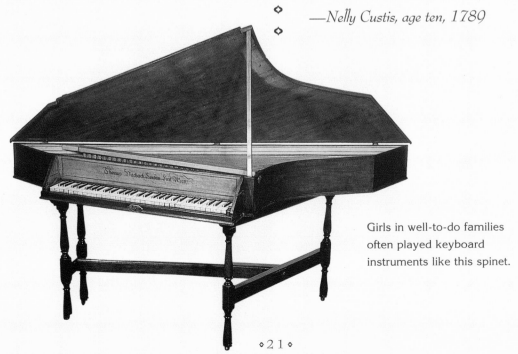

Girls in well-to-do families often played keyboard instruments like this spinet.

A Young Nation Grows

Nelly Custis once described her young self as "rattlepated . . . and giddy." A girl in a later era might have used the words "scatterbrained" and "silly." Children in the late 1700s were expected to try to outgrow such qualities quickly.

After all, this was the "Age of Reason" (a time when people began to trust science to explain the world). People had confidence that knowledge would let them control nature and make life better. Knowledge equaled progress.

One signer of the Declaration of Independence, Benjamin Franklin, had once complained that the British thought of Americans as "yahoos" (rude, stupid creatures). After the revolution, that image changed. As Americans jumped wholeheartedly into the Age of Reason, educational groups called societies sprang up all around the country. Societies encouraged the study of agriculture, medicine, math, and other fields. One French visitor grumbled that Americans thought "no one has any brains, except in America."

Nelly *(left)* and Young Wash *(right)* grew up during the Age of Reason. These 1785 portraits of them hung in their grandparents' bedroom.

WILLIAM AND BEN FRANKLIN

Many people know that Benjamin Franklin used a kite to prove that lightning is an electrical charge. Fewer people remember that Franklin's son William helped with the experiment. The two of them carried a kite out into a thunderstorm. William helped his father to get the kite to fly. When Franklin touched a key tied to the kite and got a shock, they knew they had made an important discovery. Throughout the Age of Reason, people were fascinated by scientific experiments like this one.

William Franklin and his famous father, Benjamin Franklin

Americans did feel a bit full of themselves. They'd tamed a wilderness. They'd established a brand-new nation in which they governed themselves. They believed they were free of the snobbery of Europe's class system.

And the population was growing fast. In 1790 the new nation took a census (a count of the population). "We may safely say," wrote Thomas Jefferson, the author of the Declaration of Independence, "we are above four million [people]." That same year, Philadelphia

A Mohawk village. Native Americans were not counted in the 1790 census. The census did count about 754,000 African Americans. Nearly 90 percent of them were slaves. Most slaves worked as farmhands, servants, and craftsmen.

boasted 42,500 people. It was named the temporary capital of the United States until a new capital city could be built.

People were moving west and settling new areas. Vermont became a state in 1791, Kentucky in 1792, and Tennessee in 1796.

Small communities and big cities like New York, Philadelphia, and Boston were prospering. In villages and towns all across the new nation, people lived without running water. They went to the bathroom in a privy house in their backyard. They hauled buckets of water from their wells, then emptied the dirty water into the street or yard. A fireplace or Franklin stove heated their homes in winter. Even New York City and Philadelphia lacked paved streets. People threw garbage in the gutters. Pigs squealed and rooted for leftovers. But almost every community had churches, shops, and a school. Some even had theaters and libraries. In 1789 New York had 22 churches and 131 taverns.

British Territory

U.S. Territory

Part of Massachusetts
Vermont

New York

New Hampshire

Massachusetts

Mississippi River

U.S. Territory

Pennsylvania

Rhode Island

Connecticut

New Jersey

Delaware

Maryland

French Territory

Virginia

Kentucky

North Carolina

ATLANTIC OCEAN

Tennessee

South Carolina

Spanish Territory

U.S. Territory

Georgia

The UNITED STATES in 1800

Spanish Territory

Americans were proud of their nation and celebrated their own holidays. No other nation celebrated the Fourth of July, Washington's Birthday, and Constitution Day. And Americans did them up right with fireworks, speeches, feasts, and parades. If this wasn't progress, what was?

CHAPTER THREE

Rushing
through
BABYHOOD

"If you give a child what he cries for, you pay him for crying."

—John Wesley, Methodist minister, 1780s

◇ ◇

A generation before the new nation was formed, a little girl remembered only as Sarah was born. Her mother wrapped her in swaddling clothes (tightly wound bands of cloth). Swaddling made Sarah look like a tiny mummy. It kept her stretched out straight, even when she was sleeping. Swaddling was supposed to help Sarah grow up straight and tall.

At six months, Sarah was too old for swaddling. So she wore a stiff corset around her middle to keep her back straight. She wasn't allowed to crawl. Only animals crawled! To keep her upright, her parents stuck her in a standing stool (a little chair) with her legs dangling through a hole in the middle.

All these things would help Sarah grow into a "real" human being. Her parents wanted to rush her through babyhood as quickly as possible.

Sarah would have to work hard to become someone who could walk and talk.

◇ ◇ ◇ ◇

NEW IDEAS

By the time Sarah had become a mother herself, parents no longer raised their children in those old-fashioned ways. Up-to-date mothers paid attention to the latest ideas about child rearing. Children of the new nation enjoyed more freedom and less protection—just like the new nation itself.

Like other parents, Sarah didn't think swaddling was needed. In fact, doctors were saying that swaddling and standing stools might even slow a child's progress. So Sarah dressed her son in a loose gown so he could kick and wave his arms.

Sarah's son was free to crawl, but that didn't mean she liked to see her pride and joy roaming about on the floor like an animal. She was just waiting for him to outgrow crawling. Wise parents agreed with philosopher John Locke, who said parents shouldn't worry about "faults . . . which you know age to cure."

◇ ◇ ◇ ◇

CHILDREN GET "HARDENED"

John Witherspoon, president of a college later called Princeton University, also offered parenting advice during the Age of Reason. Witherspoon advised that children should bathe frequently in cold water. Little ones must have "liberty" from parents who carried them too much. They needed to "romp and jump about as soon as they are able." And they must breathe "free air" (outside air).

All these things would help children become "hardened" to life. Otherwise, they might grow soft or spindly like a sickly plant. A gasping youngster might protest being dipped into chilled water for a bath. But it was for his own good! Babies who got used to cold and breathed fresh air became more fit than adults softened by years of overly warm clothes and stuffy indoor air.

Parents could also harden their children by being firm. At the first sign of a baby's bad habit, parents needed to teach the child who was boss. Eight or nine months old was not too early to start. A parent

Parents believed cold baths helped children to become hardened.

who gained control early "will do more by a look of displeasure," said Witherspoon, "than another [parent] by the most passionate words, and even blows."

When children cried, they might be trying to get their own selfish ways. As John Wesley, a churchman, put it in the 1780s, "If you give a child what he cries for, you pay him for crying." The result? "He will certainly cry again."

Wesley warned that grandparents might spoil children and "should not share in the management" of them. Nelly and Wash's mother, Eleanor Custis Stuart, often fretted that Martha Washington was spoiling Nelly and Wash.

No one should make excuses for a child, saying, "My child wouldn't do that!" This only encouraged children to lie. As in earlier times, a whipping remained the usual form of "correction" for bad behavior.

A grandmother and her grandson. Parenting experts thought grandparents were too lenient.

Having few luxuries also hardened youngsters in the new nation. Most children never had their own bedroom or even their own bed. They were tucked in wherever there was room. Young Wash slept in a third-floor bedroom with his grandfather's secretary, Tobias Lear. The children of wealthy Virginia planter Robert Carter slept this way: son Benjamin with his tutor, four daughters together in one room with some servants, nephew Harry and son Robert together with Mr. Carter's male secretary.

◇ ◇ ◇ ◇

WHO IS WATCHING THE CHILD?
Before the American Revolution, children in well-to-do families were cared for by servants. By the late 1700s, however, parents heard warnings about this custom. Servants might teach a child to lie or swear. Servants might bribe children to behave—a bad habit. And servants encouraged children to keep secrets from their parents.

But if servants didn't keep fussy children quiet, who would? Parents saw nothing wrong with giving a child—even a baby—beer, wine, or gin to make it sleep. Some parents gave their children "syrups" to quiet them. They didn't realize that many syrups, made from alcohol and opium, were dangerous.

Children also faced other dangers. Accidents could happen at any time. Most homes had large open fireplaces. Boiling hot cooking pots and flames could burn children. Horses and carriages ran over little ones. Guns and gunpowder in nearly every home led to shooting accidents. Youngsters drowned in rivers and wells.

Most children never had their own bedroom or even their own bed.

Ten-year-old Henry Drinker was rescued after tumbling into an icy river in 1780. "We stripped him," wrote his mother, Elizabeth, "and after rubbing him well with a coarse towel, put on warm dry clothes, gave him some rum . . . and made him jump a rope till he sweated."

With guns and open fireplaces in the house, children often suffered accidents.

THREE YOUNGSTERS STAND THE TEST
Many children died of illness before the age of five.

Doctors could do little to help, since they didn't know what caused most sickness. Taking blood from a vein was one popular "cure." Another was giving patients strong medicines to make them vomit. These cures often did more harm than good.

Smallpox was one deadly disease that killed or scarred tens of thousands of people. "Cowpox" was a similar, but less severe, disease.

This heartbroken mother is mourning the death of a baby—
a common occurrence.

"DEAR BROTHER

You can not immagin the situation of this city. . . . They are a Dieing on our right hand & on our Left. . . . Great are the number that are Calld to the grave, and numberred with the silent Dead."

—Isaac Heston, September 19, 1793

From a letter describing a yellow fever epidemic in Philadelphia. Isaac died of the fever ten days later. The disease killed five thousand people in just a few months.

In the late 1700s, scientists developed a vaccine made from cowpox to prevent smallpox. Doctors hoped it would be safer than a vaccine made from smallpox pus. But no one knew how safe it was.

Three children of the new nation helped answer that question. In 1799 Doctor Benjamin Waterhouse gave the new cowpox vaccine to his children—five-year-old Daniel Waterhouse, Daniel's three-year-old brother, and Daniel's one-year-old sister. Over the next two weeks, they each got the symptoms of smallpox: redness, swelling, and pain. But the symptoms were slight. Daniel was scarcely drawn away from "play more than an hour or two." The Waterhouse children had helped to prove that the cowpox vaccine was safe. Soon many Americans were vaccinated against deadly smallpox.

CHAPTER FOUR

The PATH of AMUSEMENTS

"I have often made him laugh heartily."

Even though children in the new nation had to grow up fast, they still had time for fun. At one children's party, the guests danced and played games (forgotten today) such as "Woo the Widow," "Thread the Needle," and "Pawns." The hostess served nuts, raisins, cakes, wine, and punch. Everyone behaved well. There was "no rudeness Mamma I assure you," one girl told her mother.

In winter, boys went sleigh riding and ice skating. Summer fun included fishing, racing, and playing ball with a sawdust-filled bag or pig bladder. Swimming was a summer sport carried on without any clothes. Young boys also flew kites, rolled hoops, and played with toy soldiers made of lead or tin. Older boys tested their skills at stool ball, badminton, and lawn bowling. They practiced shooting their guns at targets.

One tutor described his students' favorite pastimes: visiting neighbors, hunting ducks by the river, horseback riding, and watching the blacksmith or carpenter at work. A Massachusetts boy spent his evenings either reading or "roving about. . . which is generally the case with boys ten to twenty-one years old."

Girls usually followed quieter pastimes. They played with dolls, dishes, and puppets. They sewed doll clothes. Along with boys, they enjoyed games like chess, dominoes, backgammon, cards, dice, and the first jigsaw puzzles.

Opposite: A sleigh ride
Right: A wooden doll
from the 1700s

—*Nelly Custis, speaking of her grandfather, President George Washington*

GUILTY READING

Young people, especially girls, were not supposed to read novels. Novels told tales of duels, kidnappings, suicide, and romance. Such stories were too exciting. They would "inflame the passions," "corrupt the heart," and "pollute the imagination," according to one minister. Older girls sometimes secretly passed forbidden novels to each other.

Most people still believed, however, that amusements should not get in the way of education and work. In 1794 *New York Magazine* warned, "The path of amusement can become the Broadway to destruction."

LIBERTY IN FASHIONS

Like many other things, fashions for youngsters changed after the American Revolution. The new look gave children more freedom to run and play. It also gave them a separate identity from their parents.

In earlier times, only the youngest boys and girls dressed to move freely. Both boys and girls wore loose, ankle-length dresses.

After age five, children dressed like their parents. Girls dressed in heavy gowns and high-heeled shoes. Boys moved straight from their toddler dresses into men's breeches (pants that stopped at the knees).

Both boys and girls squeezed into tight sleeves. In order to have good posture, both might wear tight corsets around their middles. These uncomfortable clothes made it hard to move.

Fashions changed by the 1780s, when parents began reading the ideas of philosopher John Locke. He claimed tight-fitting clothes caused "short and stinking breath, ill lungs, and crookedness." Worried parents started letting their children dress like children until age ten or even older.

Tight-fitting clothes caused "short and stinking breath, ill lungs, and crookedness."
—philosopher John Locke

For girls, this meant long, loose dresses with a ribbon or simple sash tied around the waist. Even the fabric was comfortable—lightweight muslin, usually bleached snowy white. Girls' hairstyles also changed. In earlier times, wealthy girls had worn wigs and false curls, pinned to the head. Servants "powdered" wigs by poofing flour on them. In the new nation, girls let their hair flow loosely to their shoulders. Many wore bangs.

Girls still couldn't run and jump as easily as boys could in their pants. But the new fashions did let girls move more freely.

Anna Maria Cumpston wears a new-styled dress in this 1790 portrait.

Instances of Ill Manners To Be Carefully Avoided by Youth of Both Sexes

Entering a room with the hat on, and leaving it in the same manner

Passing between the fire and persons sitting at it

Whispering, or pointing in company

Contradicting your parents or strangers who are any way engaged in conversation

Laughing loudly, when in company, and drumming with feet or hands

Leaning on the shoulder or chair of another person

Throwing things instead of handing them

Lolling [leaning] on a chair when speaking or when spoken to

Distortion of countenance [making faces]

Mimicry [copying someone]

—from The Gentleman & Lady's Companion, printed by John Trumbull, 1798

Many girls joined boys in swinging on swings, shooting bow and arrows, playing with pets, and riding horses.

◇ ◇ ◇ ◇

THE "MAN-CHILD"

When a little boy started wearing boy's clothes instead of toddler dresses, his family celebrated with a "breeching" ceremony. One boy, John Neal, wrote this about his big day in 1795: "They put me into jacket and trousers; whereupon, they say I gathered up my petticoats and flung them to my sister, saying 'Sis may have these.' Being twins, we had always been dressed alike, till then; but from that time forward, I was the man-child and she—poor thing! only 'Sissy,' and obliged to wear petticoats."

Boys of the new nation were the first to wear pants that stopped at the ankle instead of the knee. Girls wore loose dresses like this one.

A major change for boys came during the 1790s. Instead of changing into men's breeches at age five, a boy put on long pants. With this fashion move, boys pulled on trousers about twenty years before their fathers traded in their breeches for pants. Long pants gave boys of the new nation a style all their own. The look separated them from toddlers, teenage boys, and adults.

CHAPTER FIVE

EVERY KIND *of* KNOWLEDGE

"'Tis quite enough for girls to know, If she can read a billet-doux [love letter]." —*John Trumbull,* The Progress of Dullness, *1772*

◇ ◇ ◇ ◇ ◇ ◇ ◇ ◇ ◇ ◇ ◇ ◇ ◇ ◇ ◇ ◇ ◇ ◇ ◇ ◇

People like the Washingtons and the Adams family placed great value on education. After all, as Benjamin Franklin wrote, the new nation needed leaders who would serve "with Honor to themselves, and to their Country."

Martha and George Washington tried to give their grandson a good education. But Mrs. Washington had to admit Young Wash didn't make very good progress. "He does not learn as much as he might, if the master [teacher] took proper care to make the children attentive to their books," she wrote.

President Washington fumed over the boy's apparent disinterest in school. When away from home, he wrote letters to Young Wash, advice flowing from the president's quill (feather) pen. "From breakfast until about an hour before dinner

Opposite: George Washington's quill pen and ink wells. *Right:* Young Wash

◇ 4 1 ◇

[lunch] . . . confine yourself to your studies," he told Wash. "Light reading . . . may amuse for the moment, but leaves nothing behind," he pointed out. Apply yourself! he was saying, "instead of running up and down stairs" seeking "anyone who will talk with you."

Even with this prodding, Young Wash chose not to work hard in school. As a young man, he flunked out of three different colleges.

Like the Washingtons, John Adams pushed his son John Quincy to study hard. As John Quincy put it, "Pappa . . . takes a great deal of Pains to put me in the right way." John Quincy tried to keep a journal of his studies, as his father asked. But he wondered whether his journal was scholarly enough. "A journal Book . . . of a Lad of Eleven years old can not be expected to contain much of science, literature, arts, wisdom, or wit," the young Adams hoped.

"A journal Book . . . of a Lad of Eleven years old can not be expected to contain much of science, literature, arts, wisdom, or wit."
—John Quincy Adams, age eleven, 1778

DAME SCHOOL
Most children of this era received their only education at home. They learned a little reading by studying from the only books in the house—a Bible or an almanac (a book of wise sayings, weather information, and other facts).

Youngsters in wealthy families learned at home, too. But often their families had libraries. Sometimes they had private tutors who lived with the family.

The dame in this dame school is punishing one boy by making
him sit in the corner wearing a dunce cap.

In small towns, some young children had the chance to attend a
"dame school." Dame schools were taught by a woman (usually an
older neighbor woman) in her home. One girl who had gone to
dame school remembered the dame drinking her tea from the teapot
spout. On some afternoons, the children waited quietly while the
dame took a nap.

Each day in a dame school began with a Bible verse. Then the
dame taught a bit of reading, spelling, and even sewing. When the
children were good, they got a drink of water from a large mug
passed around the circle. The dame kept daydreamers in line with a
sharp rap on the head with her steel thimble.

Only boys received further education. Between the ages of six and
fifteen, they attended grammar schools. These schools were also
called Latin schools, since they emphasized Latin. That language
was important in preparing a boy for college, where he could study
to be a minister, doctor, or lawyer.

MATH HEADACHES

Have you ever struggled with a math problem? Try solving this one:
Deduct the Tare and Trett. Divide the Suttle by amount given:
the Quotient will be the Cloff which subtract from the Suttle the
Remainder will be the Near.

—from a colonial arithmetic book by Nicholas Pike of Newburyport, Massachusetts

Latin schools were usually one-room buildings with a collection of benches, a stove for heat, and homemade school supplies. Students gave "recitations" (reciting lessons out loud from memory). Books were not written for different grades or ages, so the same "primer" had to do for everyone.

By 1790 Latin was taught less. Latin schools began to be replaced by education academies for boys. Academies emphasized practical studies such as math, public speaking, logic, surveying, drafting, writing, and sciences such as biology and physics.

SCHOOLMASTERS

Just as most students were boys, most teachers were men. The job offered low pay and little status. Some teachers were educated. Others could barely read or write.

Teachers in Latin schools faced students of all ages. Some were older than the teacher. Every class seemed to have bullies. In one sport, called "turning the master out," the biggest boys carried the teacher outside and dumped him in the schoolyard.

Not surprisingly, many teachers ruled through fear. Offenses such as lying, laughing, leaving your seat, or giving a bad recitation earned a punishment. Sometimes teachers whipped students with leather straps or made them carry heavy blocks of wood until their arms ached. Some teachers dragged offenders about by their ears until the skin was torn and bloody.

"He tries, with ease and unconcern, to teach, what ne'er himself could learn."
—*John Trumbull,* The Progress of Dullness, *1772*

In one Massachusetts school, boys were struck on the flat of their hands with a rod. The number of strikes could be "from 2 to 4 up to 1 or 2 dozen, according to the nature of the offense & the size of the boys," one boy wrote. The hitting hurt. "A few of the older boys never cried, but only changed colour violently as the blows fell: but the other boys always cried."

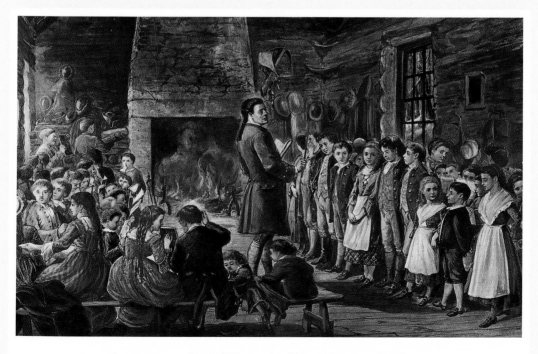

A one-room school. Girls received less education than boys.

EDUCATING A YOUNG LADY

At least half of the new nation's women could not read. In most poor families, girls received little or no book learning. In wealthy families, though, some girls had tutors or attended academies for young ladies. Nelly Custis attended one fashionable new girls school—Mrs. Graham's School—in New York. No one dreamed a young woman might go to college.

Girls didn't need book learning for their future jobs as wives, mothers, and housekeepers. So schooling for girls focused on politeness and other social skills. Girls studied homemaking, sewing, embroidery, and French instead of math, science, or geography. Thomas Jefferson believed America's future depended on educated citizens. But for his daughter, Martha, he outlined studies of dancing, drawing, music, and letter writing.

Girls trained to be housewives. Boys had more options.

Patty Polk practiced stitching a sampler similar to this one.

"Patty Polk did this [sewing] and she hated every stitch she did in it. She loves to read much more."
—*Patty Polk, 1800*

People thought too much education could even be harmful to girls. Schooling would give them "monstrous brains and puny bodies." One reverend declared, "As for training young ladies through a long intellectual course, as we do young men, it can never be done. They will die in the process."

Some girls rebelled as best they could. In 1800 one young lady practiced her sewing by cross-stitching these words: "Patty Polk did this and she hated every stitch she did in it. She loves to read much more."

AMERICAN MADE

Most books in the colonies had been published in England. But Americans in the new nation wanted their children to learn from American books. "America must be as independent in literature as she is in politics," wrote Noah Webster in 1783.

Webster's words introduced one of the earliest American schoolbooks, a blue-covered spelling book. Until then, Americans

"Can't Tell a Lie, Pa"

Instead of reading books for pleasure, children in the new nation were encouraged to learn valuable life lessons through reading. One best-selling book was *The Life of Washington*. The author, Mason Locke Weems, was a parson. In the book, he invented a useful story about the childhood of the country's first president.

According to Parson Weems, six-year-old George Washington was given a new hatchet and tested it against his father's prized cherry tree. George's father soon discovered the splintered trunk and questioned the household. Finally, George's father asked George, "Do you know who killed that beautiful little cherry-tree yonder in the garden?" As Parson Weems wrote:

> This was a tough question; and George staggered under it for a moment. . . . [Then] he bravely cried out, "I can't tell a lie, Pa; you know I can't tell a lie. I did cut it with my hatchet." "Run to my arms, you dearest boy. . . ," cried his father, "glad am I, George, that you killed my tree; for you have paid me for it a thousand fold."

Like most stories children heard, this one taught a lesson. It inspired children to follow the example of the great George Washington by telling the truth.

> *"I have read my Bible to my aunt this morning (as is the daily custom) & sometimes I read other books to her."*
>
> *—Anna Green Winslow, a schoolgirl in Boston, Massachusetts, writing in her diary, February 9, 1772*

THE
AMERICAN
SPELLING BOOK;

CONTAINING,

THE RUDIMENTS
OF THE
ENGLISH LANGUAGE,
FOR THE
USE OF SCHOOLS
IN THE
UNITED STATES.

BY *NOAH WEBSTER*, ESQ.

JOHNSON'S SECOND REVISED IMPRESSION.

PHILADELPHIA:
PUBLISHED BY JACOB JOHNSON & CO.
NO. 147, MARKET-STREET.
1804.

Noah Webster's spelling book

did not have a standard way of spelling. Using Webster's book, students learned to spell by saying one word at a time out loud. Everyone learned the same spelling.

Webster soon added a grammar book and reading book to the short list of American schoolbooks. His book *The Little Reader's Assistant* taught American history and government, "adapted to the capacities of children." Other American authors added math and geography books. For the first time, schoolchildren were learning from books by American authors—and published in America.

CHAPTER SIX

Bright
PROSPECTS

"I have never seen in this Country a Beggar such as I used Daily to see in England."

—an Englishman's comment when visiting the new nation, 1770s

In 1800 the average age of Americans was only sixteen. Families were often large—eight to ten children was common. To save money and space, parents encouraged youngsters to leave home early and earn their own way.

Since the new nation had so few people and so many natural resources, there was plenty of opportunity to go around. Children didn't have to learn the trade of their father or hope they would inherit land. Down the river, or over the mountain ridge, there was always good land a young person could claim for his own. One Englishman observed, "I have never seen in this Country a Beggar such as I used Daily to see in England."

◇ ◇ ◇ ◇

ATTENDING TO DUTIES

In 1795 Asa Sheldon of Massachusetts "made a contract" with a livestock owner. The man would pay Asa to herd his cattle and sheep while the man ate breakfast. Asa Sheldon, businessman, was seven years old.

Before long Asa was earning money by plowing fields for a local farmer. Around age eleven, he left home ("an important event in the history of a youth," he said) and became a farmer's apprentice. As an apprentice, Asa helped with the farmer's work. In return, he lived with the farmer's family and learned how to farm.

To arrange this, the farmer paid Asa's father twenty dollars. The farmer also promised to give Asa one hundred dollars when the lad turned twenty-one. But the farmer treated Asa unfairly, so Asa left before his twenty-first birthday.

Like Asa, many youngsters became apprentices by age twelve, thirteen, or fourteen. Sometimes they went to work for older brothers or sisters or other family members. A boy might help an uncle with his business. A girl could join her cousins as a baby-sitter. Sometimes fathers made work contracts with their own children.

Other children ended up working for strangers. A father might sign up an eight-year-old son as a cabin boy on a trading ship. Some fathers sent their children to cities to work in textile mills.

Most children worked to learn a trade or skill. But some were forced to work for other reasons. With little medical knowledge and poor sanitation, sickness and death struck most families. Only 20 percent of mothers survived to see their youngest child grown up. If both parents died, children grew up as orphans and had to make their own way.

Families with money tried to give their children "a start in life" by granting them money, land, or a good education. Older boys went to live with tutors or to stay at schools far away from home.

John Quincy Adams trained to follow in his father's footsteps as a diplomat and politician. In 1778, at age ten, he left his mother behind and sailed to France with his father, a diplomat.

A shoemaker's apprentice and his master

Like other Virginia planters, the Washingtons owned slaves.

A Life of Work and Worry

For slave children in the new nation, childhood ended early. Many had to work alongside their parents by age eight.

One slave girl, remembered only as Sally, lived in a rickety wooden cabin where wind blew in, and damp and snow seeped inside. A heap of straw with a blanket was her bed. Year-round, day and night, Sally wore the same dress. She and her family filled their hungry stomachs every day with cornbread and a bit of pork. In summer they grew vegetables in a garden behind the cabin.

Sally's father was owned by a different man. Once a week he walked six miles to visit his family. Sally's master sold her brother, and the family didn't know where he was. Every day Sally worried that her mother would be sold—or she would be sold herself.

At age twelve, he traveled on a year-long mission with diplomat Francis Dana, working as Dana's secretary. Young Adams returned to America and entered Harvard College in 1785.

◇ ◇ ◇ ◇

BEHAVING LIKE A WOMAN

The moment came for every girl when she had to look and act like a woman. By age fourteen, girls gave up their loose dresses and laced into women's tight dresses and corsets. In 1793 Elizabeth Ham stood on a window seat in her home to be measured for her first corset. After a few weeks of wearing it, she wondered whether the "advantage of a fine shape" was worth what she called the "punishment." People thought it important for girls to look attractive, since they were expected to catch a husband.

Older girls also wore their hair like their mothers—pulled up and pinned with combs. The first day Lucy Larcom wore her hair pulled up, she had "a good cry." It was her "duty to think and behave like a woman," she wrote in her diary. The trouble was, she still "felt like a child."

It was her "duty to think and behave like a woman."
—*Lucy Larcom, early 1800s*

A girl laced her corset tightly to make her waist tiny.

To European visitors, though, America's spirited young ladies seemed to have a lot of freedom. One writer noted that "female children rejoice" when they were old enough (at age twelve or thirteen) to be called "Misses." Young ladies "enjoy all the privileges of self-management," he noticed. Another visitor, a Frenchman named St. Me'ry thought American girls enjoyed "unlimited liberty."

◇ ◇ ◇ ◇

COURTING

A young man who wanted to win the hand of a liberty-minded young lady had to court her. Even in America, though, young couples were seldom left alone together. Courtship took place under a family's watchful eye.

People in the new nation loved music. Dancing was the most popular form of socializing. So, many young people courted as they

Settlers in small homes and one-room cabins danced to music by instruments that were often homemade.

danced at parties till the sun rose. In the parlors of the rich, they stepped through stately dances called minuets. At a clearing in the woods, they clapped and stomped to a rousing jig or reel.

Since dancing helped a child attract a suitable marriage partner, learning how to dance was serious business. Some wealthy families even hired dancing masters. A tutor on a Virginia plantation (large farm worked by slaves) remembered that everyone gathered in the "Dancing-Room" after breakfast one day. According to him, the dancing master "struck two of the young Misses for a fault in the course of their performance, even in the presence of the Mother of one of them!"

Courting couples sipped tea and ate cakes together. Young gentlemen rowed their fair ladies along gentle streams. On the western frontier, young adults mingled at barn raisings, harvest celebrations, and corn-shucking bees. Couples exchanged love letters when apart.

Young people flirted at harvest celebrations and other gatherings.

"Oh, My Heart!"

Sally Wister enjoyed the attentions of some of the officers who stayed with her family in 1777. She wrote a friend about one in particular—the army paymaster. He had a "beautiful glow to his cheeks" and lovely windblown hair. "Oh, my heart, thought I," Sally wrote, "be secure!"

Sally dressed carefully to impress her male admirers. When a visitor caught her one day in her plain work dress, she got upset. She noted that men could be just as vain, though. "If they have a fine pair of eyes, they are ever rolling them about;" she wrote, "a fine set of teeth, they are great laughers. . . . Oh, vanity, vanity!"

Marriage

Usually young people in the new nation chose a husband or wife based on love. But love was not always considered. Wealthy families, especially in the South, often arranged marriages for their children. They made sure their child married a rich partner, not someone poor.

Sometimes young people rebelled against an arranged marriage. Some ran away together without permission. Choosing an unsuitable husband or wife meant a girl or boy could be cut off from the family.

Before getting married, rich sons usually waited to finish their education or start a career. Poorer couples married younger—there was always land to support them if they worked hard.

> *"A sensible woman can never be happy with a fool."*
> —George Washington to Nelly Custis, March 1796

As a wife, a young woman gave up the "liberties" she enjoyed as a carefree girl. The Frenchman de St. Me'ry observed that after marriage, a woman lived "only for her husband." Her role was "to devote herself . . . to the care of her household and her home." A married women had no right to own any property, no right to keep any wages she earned, no right to custody of her children in case of divorce.

> *After marriage, a woman lived "only for her husband." Her role was "to devote herself . . . to the care of her household and her home."*
> —Moreau de St. Me'ry, 1790s

Since marriage was such a serious step for a woman, George Washington advised Nelly Custis to take care when choosing a mate. "When the fire is beginning to kindle, and your heart is growing warm, [ask] these questions," he wrote to her. "Is he a man of good character? A man of sense? For be assured a sensible woman can never be happy with a fool."

Nelly married on February 22, 1799—her grandfather's sixty-seventh birthday. She was twenty. Her bridegroom was Lawrence Lewis, a nephew of George Washington's. Lewis was nearly twice her age.

The following November, Nelly gave birth to a daughter. She wrote a friend that "the once rattlepated, lazy Eleanor P. Custis" had grown up. Although Nelly had once been considered "a thoughtless giddy mortal," motherhood changed her into "a sedate matron attending domestic duties and providing for a young stripling who could call her mother."

This drawing of Nelly Custis at her wedding shows her grandfather, George Washington, waiting for her to take his arm. Her grandmother, Martha Washington, is on the stairs behind Nelly.

Born during the revolution, Nelly and other young people of her time had grown up as the new nation grew up. As they changed, the country did, too. It grew from rebellious youth into a nation taking care of business, seeking its place in the world.

ACTIVITIES

Study Historical Illustrations

Many of the illustrations in this book were made between 1775 and 1800. They tell us many things about life then. The portrait of the Washington family on page 20 was painted by Edward Savage in 1796. It includes many clues about their lives. For example, Martha Washington is pointing to a map for a new capital city that was being built. It was later named Washington, D.C., after her husband. Mrs. Washington grew up in colonial America and is wearing an old-fashioned gown. Young Nelly, on the other hand, is wearing the latest fashion. Young Wash has his hand on a globe. Perhaps Edward Savage was saying that all the world was within the grasp of young Americans.

This portrait also raises questions that cannot be answered. In the background stands an unidentified African American man. Some historians believe he may be William Lee, one of George Washington's slaves. Lee fought beside Washington during the revolution. Years after this portrait was made, Washington gave Lee his freedom.

When you study a historical illustration, think about more than just what you see. Also ask questions about what you can't see. Who made the illustration? Why? Does it show people acting freely, or are they posed? Does it show a certain point of view or make viewers feel a certain way?

Try studying an illustration such as the drawing on page 10. How does it make you feel about loyalists who were fleeing their homes? Make a list of things you see, such as the forest behind the people. Write down the reasons why those things might have been included. Perhaps the inky black forest suggests that fleeing loyalists might end up in a scary place. They face an uncertain future. Now share your list with others in your class. Working together, write a short paragraph that describes the message you think the illustration was meant to send. Follow these steps again to study other illustrations in this book.

Keep a Journal

When the Wisters fled Philadelphia in 1777, teenager Sally Wister missed her good friend Debby Norris. Sally couldn't talk to Debby by phone or e-mail, of course. Often she couldn't even mail a letter. To share her thoughts with Debby, Sally wrote them in a journal. Pretend that you are living during the American Revolution. Write a journal entry telling your best friend how your family is affected by the war. Have you decided to join the patriots, support the loyalists, or remain neutral? What dangers are involved? Does your family still have relatives living in Great Britain? Will your father's business be hurt if he chooses one side over the other?

Write an Etiquette Book

Take another look at the *Instances of Ill Manners To Be Carefully Avoided by Youth of Both Sexes* on page 38. Are any rules from the 1700s still useful today? What five rules would you write in a book of manners for modern times? You might include rules such as, "When calling someone on the telephone, always say your name to identify yourself." What would someone two hundred years in the past think about your rules? What would someone two hundred years in the future think?

Track Your Time

After the American Revolution ended in 1783, eleven-year-old Patsy Jefferson's father, Thomas Jefferson, asked her to follow this schedule each day:

From 8 to 10 o'clock: Practice music.

From 10 to 1: Dance on one day and draw another.

From 1 to 2: Draw on the day you dance, and write a letter the next day.

From 3 to 4: Read French.

From 4 to 5: Exercise yourself in music.

From 5 till bedtime: Read English, write, etc.

What does this schedule show about Patsy's life? Make a schedule showing how you spend your day. How does your schedule compare with Patsy's?

SOURCE NOTES

10 Milton Meltzer, editor, *The American Revolutionaries: A History in Their Own Words, 1750–1800* (New York: Thomas Y. Crowell, 1987), 164.

11 Thomas Jefferson, quoted in Meltzer, 149.

13 Sally Wister, *Sally Wister's Journal, A True Narrative, 1777–1778*, ed. Albert Cook Myers (Philadelphia, PA: Ferris and Leach, 1902), 81.

13–14 Ibid., 28.

Ibid., 81.

16 Rebecca Silliman, quoted in Linda Pollack, *A Lasting Relationship: Parents and Children over Three Centuries* (Hanover, NH: University Press of New England, 1987), 58.

17 A petition by nineteen slaves, quoted in Stanley I. Kutler, *Looking for America: The People's History* (San Francisco, CA: Canfield Press, 1976), 121.

19 Francis Hopkinson, quoted in Russell Blaine Nye, *The Cultural Life of the New Nation, 1776–1830* (New York: Harper & Brothers, 1960), 55.

21 George Washington Parke Custis, quoted in David L. Ribblett, *Nelly Custis, Child of Mount Vernon* (Mount Vernon, VA: Mount Vernon Ladies' Association, 1993), 26.

21 Nelly Custis, quoted in Richard Norton Smith, *Patriarch: George Washington and the New American Nation* (New York: Houghton Mifflin Co., 1993), 25.

21 Nelly Custis, quoted in Smith, 337.

23 Thomas Jefferson, quoted in Doris and Harold Faber, *The Birth of a Nation: The Early Years of the United States* (New York: Charles Scribner's Sons, 1989), 7.

27, 29 John Witherspoon, quoted in Philip J. Greven Jr., *Child-Rearing Concepts, 1628–1861* (Itasca, IL: F. E. Peacock, 1973), 60.

28 John Locke, quoted in Karin Calvert, *Children in the House: The Material Culture of Early Childhood, 1600–1900* (Boston, MA: Northeastern University Press, 1992), 60.

28 John Witherspoon, quoted in Greven, 84.

29 Pollock, 94.

33 Isaac Heston, quoted in Kutler, 146.

33 Doctor Benjamin Waterhouse, quoted in Logan Clendening, compiler, *Source Book of Medical History* (New York: Dover Publications, 1960), 302.

34 Nelly Custis, quoted in Smith, 25.

35 Anna Green Winslow, quoted in Pollock, 155.

35 Silas Fenton, quoted in Joseph Kett, *Rites of Passage: Adolescence in America 1790 to the Present* (New York: Basic Books, 1977), 40.

36 Nye, 146.

37 John Locke, quoted in Calvert, 82.

39 John Neal, quoted in Calvert, 85.

41 John Trumbull, quoted in Nye, 168.

41 Benjamin Franklin, quoted in Nye, 154.

41 Martha Washington, quoted in Smith, 196.

41–42 George Washington, quoted in Smith, 292.

42 John Quincy Adams, quoted in Alice Morse Earle, *Child Life in Colonial Days* (1899; reprint, Stockbridge, MA: Berkshire House, 1993), 169.

44 Nicholas Pike, quoted in Earle, 145.

45 Trumbull, quoted in Nye, 164.

45 Noel Rae, editor, *Witnessing America: The Library of Congress Book of Firsthand Accounts of Life in America, 1600–1900* (New York: The Stonesong Press, 1996), 83.

47 Patty Polk, quoted in Ethel S. Bolton and Eva Coe, *American Samplers* (1921; reprint, New York: Dover, 1987), 96.

47 Nye, 168.

47 Noah Webster, quoted in Nye, 239.

48 Mason Locke Weems, quoted in "The Papers of George Washington," The University of Virginia, <http://www.virginia.edu/gwpapers/documents/weems>.

49 Anna Green Winslow, *The Diary of Anna Green Winslow, A Boston School Girl in 1771*
     (Bedford, MA: Applewood Books, 1997), 15.
50 Rae, 41.
51 Asa Sheldon, quoted in Kett, 21.
54 Elizabeth Ham, quoted in Calvert, 86.
54 Lucy Larcom, quoted in Calvert, 87.
55 St. Me'ry, quoted in Nye, 138.
56 Rae, 339.
57 *Sally Wister's Journal*, 123.
57 Ibid., 126.
57 George Washington, quoted in Ribblett, 29.
58 St. Me'ry, quoted in Nye, 138.
58 George Washington, quoted in Ribblett, 29.
58 Nelly Custis, quoted in Smith, 337.

SELECTED BIBLIOGRAPHY

Calvert, Karin. *Children in the House: The Material Culture of Early Childhood, 1600–1900.* Boston,
     MA: Northeastern University Press, 1992.
Faber, Doris, and Harold Faber. *The Birth of a Nation: The Early Years of the United States.* New
     York: Charles Scribner's Sons, 1989.
Meltzer, Milton, ed. *The American Revolutionaries: A History in Their Own Words, 1750–1800.* New
     York: Thomas Y. Crowell, 1987.
Pollock, Linda. *A Lasting Relationship: Parents and Children over Three Centuries.* Hanover, NH:
     University Press of New England, 1987.
Rae, Noel, ed. *Witnessing America: The Library of Congress Book of Firsthand Accounts of Life in America,
     1600–1900.* New York: The Stonesong Press, 1996.
Smith, Richard Norton. *Patriarch: George Washington and the New American Nation.* New York:
     Houghton Mifflin Co., 1993.
Wister, Sally. *Sally Wister's Journal, A True Narrative, 1777–1778.* Edited by Albert Cook Myers.
     Philadelphia, PA: Ferris and Leach, 1902.

FURTHER READING

Ferris, Jeri Chase. *Remember the Ladies: A Story about Abigail Adams.* Minneapolis, MN: Carolrhoda
     Books, 2001.
Ferris, Jeri Chase. *Thomas Jefferson: Father of Liberty.* Minneapolis, MN: Carolrhoda Books, 1998.
Freedman, Russell. *Give Me Liberty: The Story of the Declaration of Independence.* New York: Holiday
     House, 2000.
Fritz, Jean. *"Shh! We're Writing the Constitution."* New York: Putnam, 1987.
Giblin, James. *The Amazing Life of Benjamin Franklin.* New York: Scholastic, 2000.
Library of Congress. *America's Story.* <http://www.americastory.gov>
Mount Vernon Ladies' Association. *George Washington's Mount Vernon.* <http://www.mountvernon.org/>
O'Hara, Megan, ed. *A Colonial Quaker Girl: The Diary of Sally Wister, 1777–1778.* Minnetonka,
     MN: Blue Earth Books, 2000.
Ribblett, David L. *Nelly Custis: Child of Mount Vernon.* Mount Vernon, Virginia: Mount Vernon
     Ladies' Association, 1993.
Streissguth, Tom. *Benjamin Franklin.* Minneapolis, MN: Lerner Publications, 2002.
Weidt, Maryann N. *Revolutionary Poet: A Story about Phillis Wheatley.* Minneapolis, MN: Carolrhoda
     Books, 1997.

INDEX